Quiet Song
A Christian Poetry Book

Elizabeth Rhodes

RESOURCE *Publications* • Eugene, Oregon

QUIET SONG
A Christian Poetry Book

Wipf & Stock
An Imprint of Wipf and Stock Publishers
199 W. 8th Ave., Suite 3
Eugene, OR 97401

www.wipfandstock.com

PAPERBACK ISBN: 979-8-3852-7369-0
HARDCOVER ISBN: 979-8-3852-7370-6
EBOOK ISBN: 979-8-3852-7371

To my mom, who always told me
to never stop writing

Dear reader,

This book started with "Things Undone," which stemmed from the depression that I experienced. I wanted to write something true, yet with a spiritual perspective. Because even in my weakest moments, God was there. So as time went on, so did the poems fall on the page, with hope, sorrow, and prayer, piecing together things that God has done.

Through hope, Jesus gives life and salvation, and he has created a world where there are moments of pure bliss and beauty. Sometimes it feels as if it's hard to capture that wonder, but it's there if you seek it. He is there if you seek him.

For sorrow, it can feel overwhelming, and darkness can sometimes be like a beautiful yet treacherous companion that we sometimes seek and fall into. However, it can also be a trap, a rope that ties us down, and occasionally outside forces cause these binds of pain, while at other times we can even cause them ourselves.

That is why prayer is so essential, that we lift our hands to God in surrender. Prayer is not just an ask, but also a time for praise and reflection. It's a conversation with God that can lead us closer to Him—basking in his comfort and finding forgiveness from our loving Father.

Yes, all these wonders of life can be explored, and I hope, with all that I have, that these words will encourage you and allow your mind to embark on this journey. And if you haven't taken a walk, step outside and feel the beauty that is the earth, because no matter where you are, beauty can be found.

Love Elizabeth

Hope

Sorrow

Prayer

Hope

But I will hope

continually, and praise

you yet more and more.

Psalms 71:14

What I've Learned About Beauty

Grass mountains,
classroom window seat,
meadow with lost deer,
notebook dog-eared.
Silkworms dance from oak trees,
hear the bell ring.
College taught me the sublime
shakes the soul like railroad tracks.
I project myself under the wheels
of that fat locomotive
to find I could hear the whistle,
collapse, a shattered jar in front
of the landscape.
Lucky to have seen quilt of yellow,
green hills, careless clouds
shape me as casually as the wind
moving the grass, or carefully, as the roots
break the pavement.

Dead-End Road

Spruce and pines are endless
needles fallen,
sap on rocks.

Ivy climbing up hills,
too many days
inside.

I forget about my body,
bread, sleep, words
enclose me.

Crow on the telephone pole,
cat nap on white leaves
shortcuts,

paths repeat, curve roads.
It would have been
too dark

to walk through at night alone.
The swing set color of
blue sherbet.

Dog that barks, I recognize they
bite people's faces
straight off.

A walk that said outside world
has been waiting,
God calling

you to leave the comfort
by the living trees
or even the dead

one beside me, branches naked
webs, strings of them
flicker in the sun.

To never find the end of the road
warning sign that says
not a through street.

In the Evening

In bed
 I think about little iron chairs facing grass slopes
garden room, ivory cushions
  sun slanted on the wood.

In bed
 I think about us taped to this place   a scrapbook,
words, a million leaves   eyes roaming   a bee,
   scarlet robe removed   by grace.

Passing thoughts under my bedroom window
      will take   a slow
heavy but calm breath.

Palm dancing over the lavender placed in a vase,
     feet gathered firmly under,
back pushed against the iron rose.

All the light in the world, from heaven
      will not witness such a small moment,
but I will.

I will lean in for every silent and spoken thought
       because these are gifts. Iron
chairs meant to be taken   to wait for God.

Yourself

Give me some impression
of your raw self,

the one who used to live in a treehouse,
play pirate,

drink solely from faucets
during summer,

pretend sleep,
sink into the magic of cloth and bedtime stories.

There is nothing more I plead,
beg you to know me.

See the butterflies pouring
from my lips, because you are youth.

Dew from the fog in the morning, so I desire
to match your breath, become myself as well.

To play like the dragonflies
over water,

daffodils swaying in the fields of imagination green.
My head swervingto look at you. To see you.

For we were
saved in this
hope, but
hope that is
seen is not
hope, for why
does one still
hope for what
he sees?

Romans 8:24

Reached for Us

On the edge of a rock,
pine huddle
at my feet;

sun making her way
beneath the bold body
of the mountain.

Blessed is the eagle's screech
mirroring the
boundless larimar sky.

I become a pine needle,
a cinder to the
cavalier universe.

To the spaceman who has seen too much,
the black hole
a telescope for God,

suspended a ball on a string.
Yet breath becomes
a spiritual donation,

a hand-me-down from God
and we look like Him,
talk like Him,

feel the scope from palms to stars,
a gap so paralyzing,
a thought forgotten

that even God wept.
Broke open the sky
reached for us.

Most Beautiful

Her father placed her mother's
ashes in Blackfoot River, pants cupped to his knees,
knuckles white and cold,
rows of Gold Larch, river rocks
at the bottom of his feet.
The Blackfoot tribe believed in sun gods.
White wolves in dreams, buffalo
to keep their stomachs full and backs warm.
What is the most beautiful thing you've seen?
Was it the moment his brother came back from the dead,
replenished, risen from a room full of ocean,
a mother breaking her body to bring another into the world,
vast plains of grain and sky--no clouds. Only sky
and your imagination.
The most beautiful thing I've seen
was alone on a mountain in the summer,
sunset of bruised blues, purples, God's
hands raising my heart in my chest.
I needed that moment to be beautiful.

God Knows

From the plane to Chiang Mai,
miles as the droplets of the
Pacific Ocean.
He's been watching the silver rim
of the blue mountains,
smoke billowing out of the mouth of the moon,
red sun, burning fire before night.

The pierced moment of gold Buddha, knees down,
incense flowing in and out of the mouths of tourists.
I cannot help but think of the songthaew,
a backdrop of rain and yellow lights. God still sees
even the baby on the chest of his Father
on a moterbike.

The Astronaut

saw the celestite line of the atmosphere,
                curve of the horizon
lying in space, this is not a sin

but a requirement to recognize
                this is beyond the human mind
of pearls, peaches, colors never seen on earth.

Magellanic clouds, Andromeda Galaxy,
                steady lights, so subtle
earth so fragile, work of art outside this window.

Patterns of a thunderstorm like neurons, tentacles,
                moving in the brain,
everything is connected; everyone hurt by the hurricane.

A terror that shifts the living being that is earth,
                the missiles seen from the
round window, separating them from life and death.

Earth opened under them, around them
                between their bodies, a space suit
blue line that covers us all, binds us together.

For since the
creation of the
world His
invisible
attributes are
clearly seen,
being
understood by
the things
that are made.
Romans 1:20

To the Palm Trees

You are most beautiful during the red cloud sky
where I'm comforted by coat and company,
the way I look up and feel poetry.
You have watched me through my steps,
my walk alone. Eyes to the sidewalk,
pupils burning into the cracks.
Each branch to where I only dream,
stretching my arm and pull
little Palm Avenue, a concrete road.
So forgive me for any hours I have wasted,
bless me for every hour I have earned.
You watched me look up, wander across,
and even though you are too tall, an amount I cannot grasp
I will still strive to see the world from your view.

Adrea Alba

Pink warmth from sunset peers through trees. Someone counted the sunflower seeds in the kitchen during dinner, and I counted them as well.
We bit down on them, stuck between our teeth, not so much pain but annoyance as if there is a jam between continents, traffic in the mouth.

Yet, I've grown from crying over the swing set and trampoline in summer, freckles on my cousin's face, bowling shoes with Sharpie, "bye," and "hi."
Sentimental for the lake with the Ardea Alba, who plucks at the fish below.
Who knows about the danger of disappearing.

I know the feeling, like I've lost the scent of the dirt path scattered with dead leaves
to my old home. Do not recall the crisp tone of my mother's calls from up the stairs,
and recently I fear I'll lose my own. God reminds me that the Ardea Alba will live forever,
that I will not face the black pit after the sunsets.

Hope Somewhere

Where do you go when the grass fields are dead?
Bare arms of birch frozen,
mountains dry from fire in the scorched canyon.
When promises lay themselves down
buried with corpses long forgotten and
copper bird nests, crown of shame.
Whose arms do you reach for when solitude is night sky,
vaster than God's garden of space, starflower.
Whom do you call when winter takes your breath,
when there is no answer
from time,
from poets,
or philosophy?
There is only a fragile view, patchy grass field
outside a pearl church.
Sometimes, the ones we least expect send prayers
like posted notes,
offerings, because they have been there once or twice as well.

Lavender Cast

Do you remember when you broke your arm?
Lavender cast with stars,
a galaxy, Milky Way on your elbow?
White socks to knees, crinkling sheets,
a click of a doctor's pen.

You cried when they wrapped those violet stars
but you cried when they took it off,
a meteor shower.
It does not take much for good to be in those fibers,
I've found He's in the tears, a mouth full of smiles

from a girl with glasses in her hair,
grin from a father embracing his son.
So much goodness can be found even in a broken arm.

Sometimes it can feel like we still wear that cast,
still see the sparkles and planets.
But we can take it off now, we can stop imagining the space above
and instead live with God, right now, with all that He is.

For every creature of God is good, and nothing is to be refused if it is received with thanksgiving.

1 Timothy 4:4

Border Between Nature and Man

Between the world of woods
and concrete.
Creatures reside there and lurk,
wet paws from streams,
eyes scan, watching me
from afar.
Battle for life while I sit
at the edge of their world

where the pavement, cracked
from undergrowth, shaken
into a new form, in wait
for the cars that no longer pass.
But once would lead
me to the house I grew up in,
the church that hurt my mother.
Music player, myself singing
in those pews, standing
in old grounds. A life between
two worlds.

Young Forgotten

All that youth, baby's breath bud,
burst out of my hands
and four black shoes carved a way into
solemn dirt paths.
Petals will crumble between our fingers,
the sweet scent,
arch of pollen on our thumbs.
When I open my eyes to tomorrow
I want to see you still standing under the rays,
your head tilted, a watering can
pouring forth, bringing life to someone.

Baptism and Her

Words-mind-vibration of sound
we whispered, and crickets chirped
in the night. The first time I felt love
from friends was on a mountaintop,
where kids immerse their heads, baptized
and when I saw the girl with doe eyes
so many years later.
How she found Christ through piercing a tattoo
of Romans on someone's skin,
I realized love is so complicated.
How I cried for this stranger
when she wore a white robe,
clean water, inside the spirit burning her
until she was all so beautiful,
a head emerged from water.

Ivory Sunflowers

Downcast sunflower,
petals, ringlets of hair falling
turned away from the Son
seeds were gathered, planted
again and again inside your heart.
You both grew, the leaves, your arms
outstretched for the Lord.
Do you know those seeds are scattered
through your laughter.
That He will never forget the garden,
dirt under nails, hurt that He's healing now.
Roots He planted you in, leading you to sprint,
shoot from the ground for His glory.
Never forget the way a flower turns its head,
away for a time of withering,
while weak, He is strong.

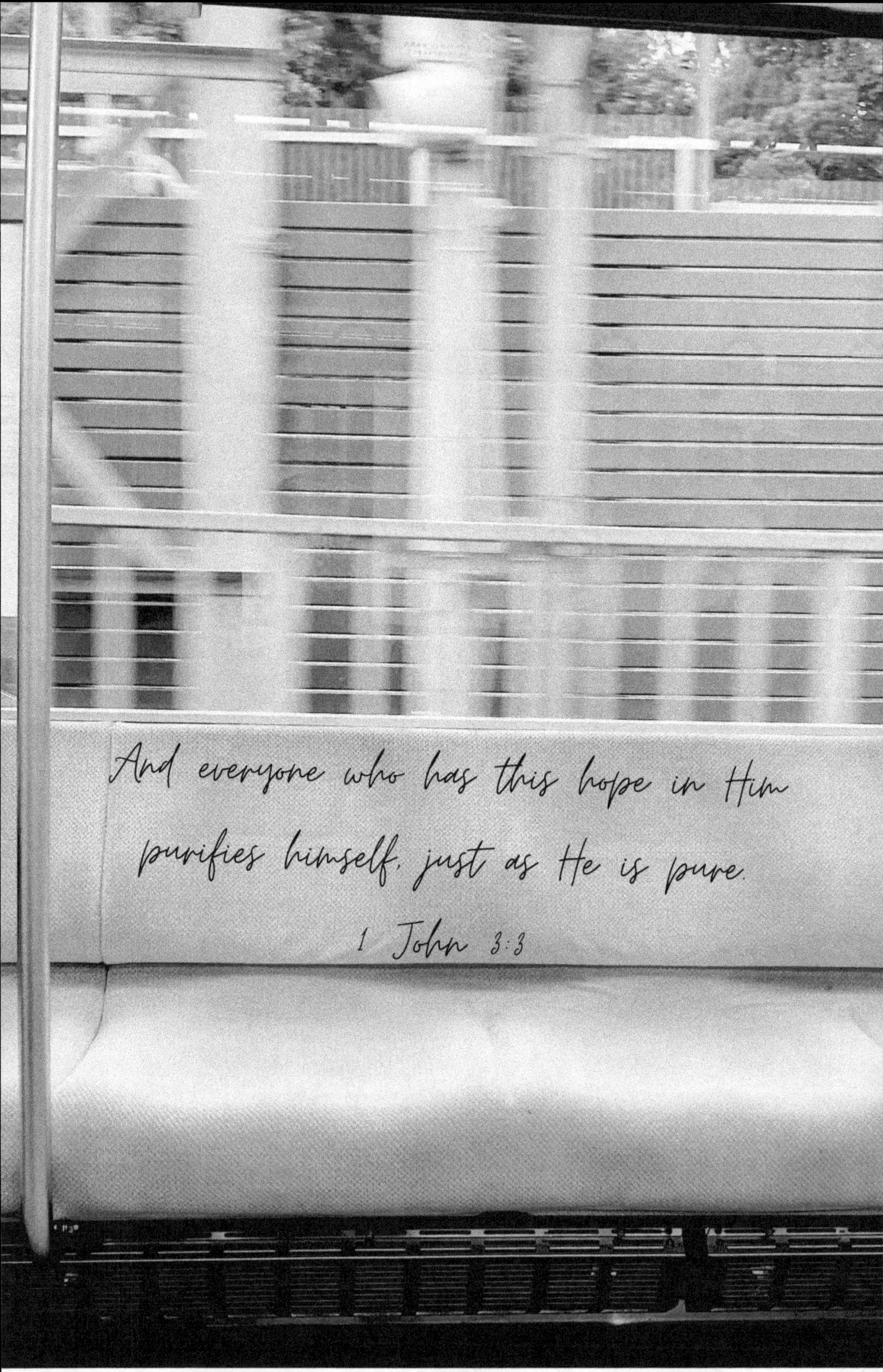

And everyone who has this hope in Him
purifies himself, just as He is pure.

1 John 3:3

Even When You First Wake

God can make us cry
while we buy our time in grocery stores.
Between the bread and milk,
check stand and receipt;
morning sky.
In the evening before you sleep,
reflection of the silver in the ocean.
The clouds cast a show,
rows of little white seats.
It's in the moment you least expect it,
brown eyes and palm trees,
dots of stars,
someone to love.
God can make us cry in many ways.

Holding Happiness

Rhythm of breath, life so given.
Hidden in copper eyes,
lies pulled like dandelions,
crimson seeds drift
in winds that know the difference
between stolen and given.
I'm holding happiness.
It's rough patches of grass
grown on roadsides,
meadows were directions
are not certain.
And Redwoods will tell tall stories
about discontentment.
I'm holding happiness
and it is by the flower eyes
opening up to me
holding me back.
How this is not achieved,
It has always been there
so welcoming yet forgotten.

Love Song

Jesus is the sweet sound of violin
the child plays in the night.
He is the breeze in the swaying desert sand,
the small acorn that is planted
in sun-bathed soil sown by a farmer.
Jesus is also in those hands
that hold the soft tan skin of a son or daughter.

Enough

You are the moment
the sun rested on lavender
and sunflower skies,
warmth pulling on
the other side
of earth.

Aurora Borealis, which has
been described as
pure happiness,
that for those few moments
the air in Iceland ceased to be cold.

You are not all happiness, not all light
and warmth, but in every moment you are
enough.

Enough to change the fragments of lives,
enough to make the very cold
in others perish.

Enough and more in ways you simply decide
to be of God.

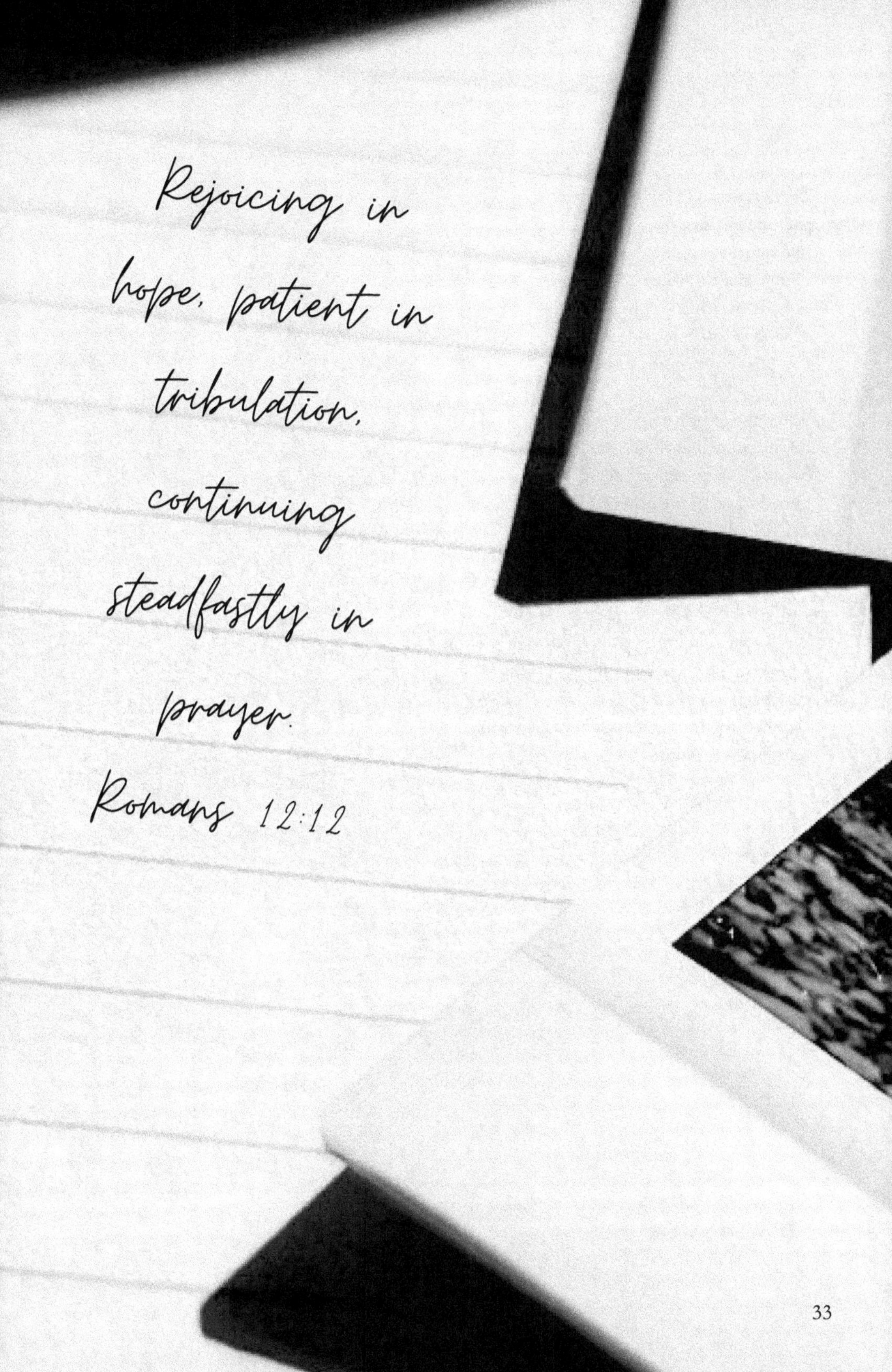
Rejoicing in
hope, patient in
tribulation,
continuing
steadfastly in
prayer.
Romans 12:12

Botanic Gardens

There is a trail in my hometown
and one in Glasgow,
I've returned to one, but I know
I'll never see foliage
cascade over me
or wooden steps
that hurt my momma's knees.

When the opportunity arises
I'll find myself at the beginning,
crossing a log that has fallen,
tipped towards the other end
and if I fall, I'll restart once again,
but I won't forget the bay, sculpted hills,
the whispers of, "I'll return."

But we know the truth. I'm looking at the fog
from a small town with dim lights at night,
a lake and a trail that I've grown up on.
Not because I want to, but because we all
return at one point.

Sweet Orchard

Like an apple, how father and mother
would cup that rotunda of a face, miss love,
spilled juice on the counter from the overflow,
burning butterflies at the bottom
of your stomach. They make figure eights, false statements.
Ink stamped with memories, but here and now Christ
holds your head, every thought fulfilled, poured
love unimagined. Reasons why this mess has been cleaned:
getting on hands and knees, rag and towel, tied to waist.
So easy for Him to wash away. To give, fold into
our shape and bind into his words, His worth is ours as well.

Joshua Tree, California

I feel the wind,
in and out the other ear
to clear, to cleanse my sins
as Jesus washes.
And the Joshua trees
huddle before the gold moment
of crisp air, silent desert, mountain rocks.

My friends and I gather, the round body
of the sun makes her performance
before our eyes. Each one thanking God
for all the little inconveniences that led us here.

Before We Sleep

Sometimes the very act of breathing, sharp, soft
low breaths before we sleep, bleed wonder of images
of here, now, and tomorrow. And all the while eyes
of a white-tailed deer, black marble
of fear has no compass or map of stars.
Instead, trust that there is meaning in the way
the deer kneels to consume wildflowers,
pants for cold Alaskan water. Believe that our breath is the intake
of God, that He let our pattern
match that of the deer, which simply desires more water.

Faith is the substance of
things hoped for, evidence
of things not seen.
Hebrews 11:1

Cathedral in Edinburgh

I waited in the cathedral to hear Scottish
accents from speakers, a thousand voices,
the mother who talks about her daughter,
and I wondered if God ever talks about me.
Maybe He murmurs my name to the angels,
dreams about me in His sleep.

God Says Lots of Things

The window should be open.
Even my cat squints her eyes — she senses it.
This room is too dark,
curtains are tanned by the sun,
marked for preservation.
Hidden inside where dishes
are undressed,
the fridge is starving.

He becomes the cold air
on my head.
All the memories of looking up
into the unfurling of cloud,
unburdened by space,
to stretch out my arms.
Choices of the beating heart
of humanity, the living creatures
that devour to survive, chirping in the
hidden trees are His birds
I do not recognize.

Sorrow

Sorrow dances before him.
Job 41:22

The Things Undone

Jesus may know I haven't
washed the dishes in bubbling soap water,
laundry unfolded and stale bread in the cupboard,
He sees the unread books, voicemails unheard.

Mostly, the bed unmade again,
my slippers. Floral robe hung
on the door.

He whispers, "Open the curtain."
The half-peek, slit of
sunlight seeks me.
I'm itching to obey.

Change with Fire

In summer,
passing mule deer, tree frogs
with crying voices
of people before, and—
as if snug in the grass
I wept to the pines.
Oh God, the—
utter destruction.
Fire suffocates,
hands around
the forest. Flames
suck the souls
out of rabbits' dens.
—Oh peace
when smoke smothered by rain
I purge, maple leaves turn black,
Blue Jay crams between the branches,
a tilted head looking into me.
I find autumn
has its own blessings, charred season,
and I am a handful braver,
understanding the erotic dance
of the flames—
the lies that brought me to my knees
and slithering snakes
jumping through the ashes,
and oh God—
watched me crawl into a hole
but I could not avoid
the heat.
But when it stopped,
I coughed up the truth.
I am not perfect,
only small and to God I should be obsolete
but still, He keeps me.

What Florance Should Know

Won't jump off a five-story parking structure onto flat, smack concrete,
or crash my car into the side of a mountain just to watch the engine sling out of its body
out of my body. Never would I plan to buy black heels and a white dress just to look nice at
my own funeral--burial--just a white ghost passing my mind before I slam on the brakes,
peeling over the edge, facing the 91 freeway.

At seventeen, I filled out a form. The therapist, who was only a few years older, curly hair
and wide waist, said, I didn't check the box that said I ever fantasized about driving off a
cliff in a cloud of smoke--my body, bread breaking--bursting like a tailpipe.

It was guilt, like in a book that I read. The author Florence said sadness is a sin. You want
to eat that little black toast, let it munch, mold into your teeth, because you can't see that
it's all a matter of the mind. Well, Florence, I did want the burnt pieces.

I didn't want to think of Jesus' body cracking like a baguette. Like his face, like all the faces,
with watered eyes--a church--a stone castle--of guilt. That said, you just need to choose. But
the man in the Bible who played the harp knew that sometimes the scabs in our heads need
some time to heal.

That bread and four-inch nails in hands can make things new, but not easier.
No, Florence, not easier.

I Know a Fake Smile

There's a forest fire in the sky,
bleeding for miles—the stretch of a life.
Last December, hibernated like a bear
in bed that looked like a cave.
Reunite with furnace, bundle with misery,
while contemplating text of, "Is this okay?"
Anytime the atmosphere is red like that,
it's in solitude, in crosswalks—parking lots,
empty football fields, head to solid ground
while the world looks upside down. Reaching
where the whole foundation could flip in an instant.
But there is a forest fire in the sky, and hands are
on arms, tug of don't fly and be burned.
There are notes—posted between doorways,
in kitchens, in living rooms, all around,
where they won't escape. Red skies that are only
reflections of a sunset. Ladders that would often
lead to flaming skies beyond.

For I am ready to fall,
and my sorrow is
continually before me.
Psalms 38:17

Fall from Grace

My grandfather nearly killed himself climbing a ladder to the roof.
It's moments like those we bring ourselves to a little altar. Slaughter our sins,
whisper in our sleep that God pulses the blood for them.
I don't know the man my grandfather was---know all
who God is. All I know is that I am selfish. My words like that ladder,

rattle, snapping bones,
I didn't even ask to hold
your hand on hospital sheets,
beg, pray you'll know me or God.

If you live to tomorrow,
forgive the shingles,
the spine of the ladder,
my open mouth
that has no voice
to warn you from
falling.

Till Sunrise

When I didn't sleep;
when I had so many possibilities
sunk inside my bed. My weight pushed the foam
down after countless hours of turns,
pulling off the sheets.
Until the very walls had begun to laugh,
TV flashed in the middle of the night, and
the big world formed inside my mind, from screens, from sirens, from
the look in the mirror that was my face.
She told me so young and shy, she told me
to cry on the sandpaper tile,
unit I worshiped the idea of sleep,
with chamomile tea, mosquito repellent circling
the air like a pill that would cure me.
She said just find comfort in these things. But I stayed awake and
at the break, I peered so hard out the window in my bedroom,
webs wrapped around the edges,
the bucket with weeds, rusting shovel.
And overhead the roofs of houses, spreading,
sliced grapefruit, a mixture of apples and oranges
a backdrop of gold sun lifting from
the dead grass.
My bones felt the heat
even behind glass.

When I'm Afraid

Wood chips on the playground,
my scraped knees like split tomato,
the seeds inside me spilling

while in winter, my skin would crack,
I'd cry in the corner with a bloody nose,
Rorschach inkblot on my napkin.

I would wait years for a man
to give me roses for the first time,
I'll wait longer for Jesus' blood to return.

Because even though I was so
afraid and yet still so afraid when I cut myself
in the kitchen, or the red in my tired eyes

when I feel less human and more human
during the confusion of traffic, stoplight
that holds my being for two seconds longer

then intended. This life is exhausting, I see
spots when I close my eyes, but I also see
the warm love so rich, so burning on my

tongue. So vibrant when I stop to listen
to the woman at the counter, the man
with the shopping cart, woman who birthed me.

My mind is stark red when God looks at me,
I hear constantly that He knows me,
with courage, break open my heart.

Struggle to Love

The deep pressure arises,
she returns. Little palms of a child
touching bare side,
dull noise of ceiling fan, creak from
a backyard door. A consistent
breath over the phone,
old onion left in the fridge for two weeks
long, in my words, "I do not want to go on."
Your silence was thunderclap, misbelief
hidden in soft words that you won't speak,
but I, red brick wall,
branches circle me. "I do not want to go on."
Why are your outstretched hands so vital to me?
How come I want to hear the sing-song voice
over the muffled connection, say
"You are not okay."
Bring me your sap, your silk words
poisoned with sun rays
uncomfortable rants
that of old mother
folds of it.

But silence.

Let me question this call. Take a deeper look at "i."
She, too, lacks the rich diet of love. Nulls at her thin body, eye of
unbecoming, lazy letter that is desperate for more--

God.

The kind of sorrow God wants us to experience leads us away from sin and results in salvation. There's no regret for that kind of sorrow. But worldly sorrow, which lacks repentance, results in spiritual death. 2 Corinthians 7

Field of Ants

Field of want
  are many weeds
burst from grounds,
  and for their desire
for water.
  Strangle any other
life.
  They build themselves,
little ants
  climb over each other's bodies,
bridges to the source,
  struggle towards
the landscape of my own want.
  What flowers have I killed
with my big brown boots
  in the garden when no one
was watching?

Lola Remember

Your brawl with English, salt, pepper hair,
rooted world in mock walnut eyes,
a Visayan spotted deer sprinting
towards open fields
away from the men who
steal hearts like wheat flour
unfurled over the mountains
and the black veil of kept secrets
of Bacuit Archipelago--*Paraiso.*
Falling in love with men in combat boots,
a dawning smile, aster in hair,
collective village, hands on the Narra tree,
lover with limestone, coral reefs,
repeating until you are left with memories
of the broken promise of once Eden.
Lola, remember that Jesus sees every
flower petal left in your hair, even after
the strong, burning remnants of lost years.

Thank God I Grew Up

There are many cries
and in a time when I stood by
Loch Katrine
skipping rocks with my mother,
ones shaped like hearts, and beside us
rose bushes, milk swans with ebony beaks.
I'm reminded of my silent voice
the one crying in bed,
moon on her pillow--
silhouette, shallowest of men
behind the bedroom curtain.
And Father, I forgive you for not loving me.
I have found a heavenly one
who pulls the white pebbles
on top of the blue morn-water
carried to shore.
And forgive me if I cried only inside
or in the secret corner of my room,
because when I was a child
I did not watch the slow crawl of the fog,
steps to understanding grace,
the cove of the eye that sees that all
things grow older but never die, never.

Morning Gray

I know that nasty December thoughts
will convince me to make coffee at two
in the morning.
Picasso's paintings, Russian ballerina,
a soloist has given his life to the leaps,
ache in his back, torn muscles.
What his body can take at age thirty-four,
and we cannot dance forever.
When the brew is done,
I'm reminded of birthday letters,
when I fell asleep and you did the laundry.
How December shifts her weight
onto the edge of my bed.
And for every reason, I should fold
myself into a question mark.
There is still another morning
that could convince me to dig myself
out of those thoughts.

The greater my
wisdom, the greater
my grief. To increase
knowledge only
increases sorrow.
Ecclesiastes 1:18

Lingering in the Dark

On the porch in the dead night alone,
I realize I'm neither young nor old—I am only

flicker of the candle wick,
a feeble light without God.

Cradle where I once wept,
memories that carry me along.

Crumble of the bread crust,
the signs I read wrong.

May God, may God, may God
Follow me down this path.

Sweater I Wore for Years

Reminds me of the starless sky, blinking streetlights on Stone Avenue.
Enfolds around my shoulders, the hood over my head.
When I take it off, months eclipse around years. I forgot the frayed fabric.

Without those fibers, the homeless man who burns his sweater in the middle of the street in downtown doesn't bother me. I'd watch the flames rise in the middle of shops with jeans that range from $50 to $90 because these are antiques.
And when my mother bought me ice cream, sitting on a park bench, my mind

was millions of miles away from the corner closet in my bedroom. From when autumn came, like a marathon when somone said, "Stay a bit longer." But I've got work in the morning. I can't handle another night with the YA group,
where I felt I had to bring my brother to bowling night because I was too shy to talk to anyone.

That sweater became cloudy sunset drives where I'd put in my headphones and cry in the back seat like I was twelve,
as if, "I'm in a hole I don't want out of," I told my mother, and she looked at me like I was an elephant sitting in her Toyota.
And all the while, the girl from YA today never remembered my name, but that's okay. That was yesterday--

I've learned to pray for others, and not just expect them to pray for me. I'm sure that sweater is still sitting in the closet,
threads dangling around each other, mixed with feelings at the time I couldn't express
a feeling of wearing too much fabric
in the hot desert, you know it's uncomfortable, but I know I still wore mine.

Even Then

I mourn a lot of things,
I mourn DVDs, finding Bambi for $1.99,
the house that kept the Christmas lights on all year
because those boys lost their mother during winter.
Late nights waiting in the car
cause mother said we'll leave in, "One minute,"
but she talked with my aunt for another thirty minutes, frost
collected on windows.

I moved away from my old town just to regress
seven years later, but I swear the trees never looked this beautiful
in autumn. A wool blanket that reminds me
my childhood was a little bit messy,
but never shocked when the lights went out in the storm,
the smoke of fire. Board game, sleeping indoors.

I am a mourning child who never knew her real father
who came to the door when she was no more than four;
what a strange man in the cold weather
and I still hold pain, waking up in the middle of the night
back aching, rolling up like smoke,
the withering away breaking—the trees change color here.

Angry Seeds

Haven't you heard that anger is a seed-----------and in my bold italicized apology
to God—Jesus, son of Nazareth-------------------Listen, God, people are so small
and people daily find themselves------------------crawling at their own walls of words
cutting others down---------------------------------- and I've read plenty of Psalms.
And my grandfather would say
How can you soar-----------------------------------as an eagle while surrounded by buzzards,
and for a long time, I pictured---------------------that people belonged at the bottom of
Jesus' sandals. But Jesus plants-------------------wonder. He does not purposely eat sunflower
seeds to watch them grow-------------------------crafting weeds inside one's belly.
He forgives the red in my--------------------------eyes—the red lines between these
grammatically incorrect--------------------sentences. And it is now a bridge. Words I walk on.

Laughter can conceal a heavy heart, but when the laughter ends, the grief remains.

Proverbs 14:13

By the Black Lake
I imagine I will recall this moment
even after I fall into a pattern of
sleeping on the couch
watching Jeopardy.
The TV a god to the elderly,
microwaved dinners, trays set up,
the glow, night awaiting
but never seeing
gentle breeze
whispers on my neck.
Tips of my fingers touch
a stone that has been aging, shaped
into a clear-cut line to show how mature it is.

I pray that when I get old, I will not wait for death
like that of my grandmother, waiting for death,
waiting for the news from the doctor, from the priest,
your lover, father, or mother. Yes, you are dying,
that of a grape, wilt and will fall off the vine and into the earth.
Yes, you are a sinner, you don't love enough, and are not loved enough.

I pray I'll never believe a word that I say. Only God's words
will be like a black lake. Constant, shimmering little water
in His hand. A view that glides oxygen into my lungs and
reminds me His love is forever. I can look at the lake forever.

Washed the Blood

If this is your last breath, I hope you breathe in the rain, waterfall,
down to the white blanket that holds your fleeting scent.

I hope you remember when you strung the Christmas lights over the fireplace,
watched a Christmas Carol, the one in color.

Pray for peace over your head as you sleep on the blue chair in the living room,
that throughout all that time you haven't grown too far

away from believing in the silver ribbon that I've seen in the clouds, a rainbow
of reasons for life. That even the woman with the basket in the street,

cigarettes, paper bags, and always smiling. She sees it too,
the sky that stretches to heaven, even in all the black clouds that

cover your head. They often covered mine too, until Jesus
polished the water off my face.

So, if this is your last breath, I'm not sorry. Sometime before you were youth
as well. You washed the blood from your younger brother's knee,

washed it when your baby girl cut her finger from paper. And watched the blood
go down the kitchen sink, the same way you think of Jesus' blood,

how it must have drained down into the core of the earth, each drop a chance.

Fear at 11:01 O'clock at Night

Glass of wine grew into my hand,
blanket around my shoulder.
The TV burned into my retina,
downward into the dirt,
lie on the floor like a dog and think.
Who is God? What is the meaning of the galaxy
that I only see through a screen?

Spider Plant

When I'm sad like this
like your goldfish, which died when you were a kid
because you didn't feed it.
I wonder why I crave poisonous stories
like the Titanic and girls locked up in loony bins.
And God knows I'll listen to crying pianos,
violins. Wrap myself up in blankets.
Match that of the screaming bobcat
my cousin and I heard coming from the night.
We told our grandfather, who brushed it off,
but we were scared. We were fading into
round vertical braid of reasoning. The cat
that it attacked is dead. And so is my sadness sometimes
when God is pounding in my chest telling me to let Him in,
and all I see is the breeding of blackberries, boysenberries,
the spider plant that my grandmother hung in her garden room.
Now that room is gone.
And I'm the spider plant, I grow and grow inside that pot
but I have no way to escape.
Only wiggle my way into praying
God, please lead me to light.

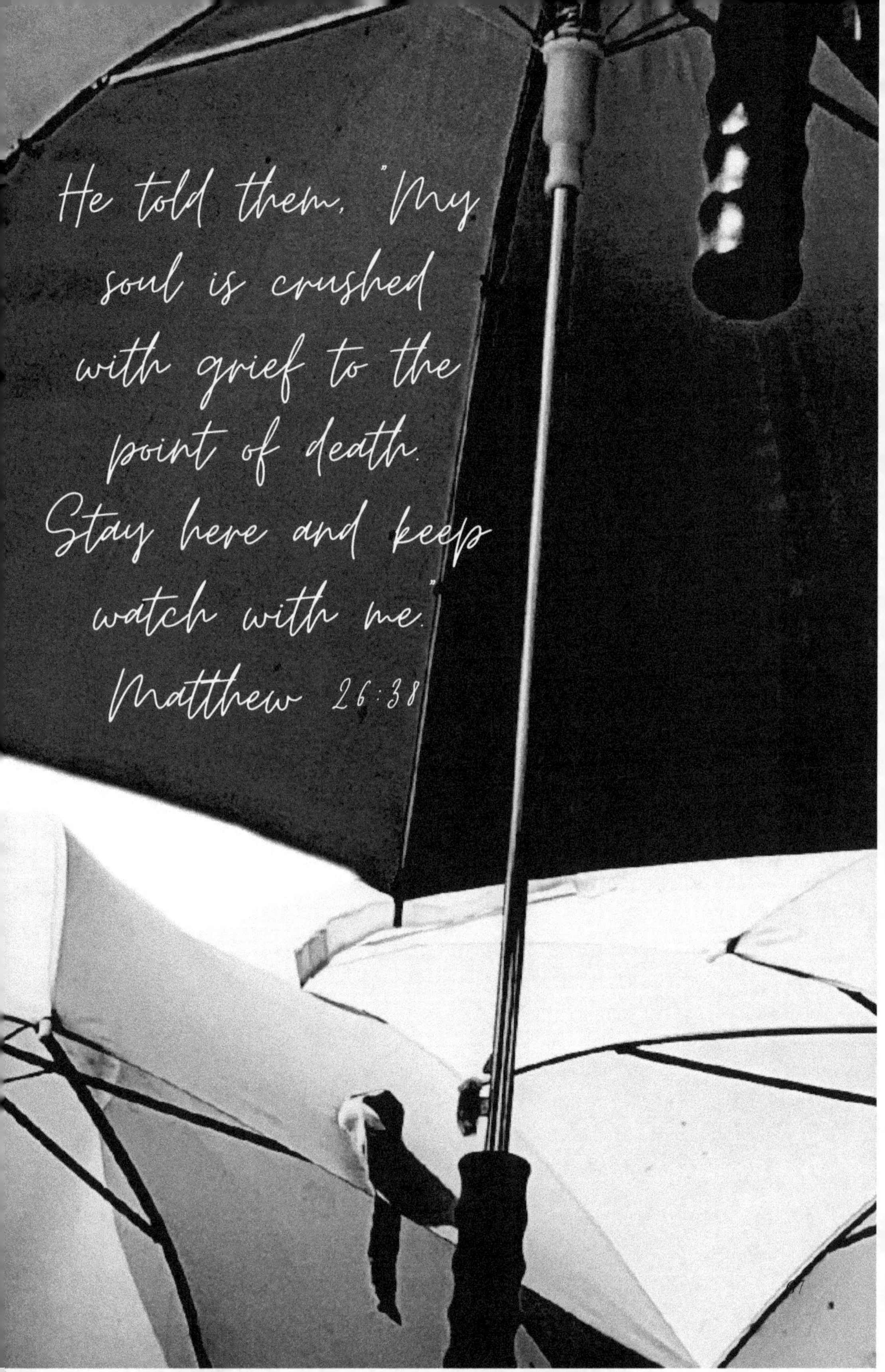

He told them, "My soul is crushed with grief to the point of death. Stay here and keep watch with me."

Matthew 26:38

I'm Sorry to Myself

I'll remember,
lost connection on the phone, the buzz,
your scream and blood on the carpet.
The relief of the firetruck,
and only a month before the house
on your street turned into
a burnt corpse.
Because the man probably left on the
stove, or dropped a cigarette.
So I'm sorry to myself,
I've learned not to weep
when there is trouble,
and Jesus helps me to pray
He'll save your soul.
I'm weary, maybe like the cracks
in the black house,
what's left of it.
I'm tired of you not wanting to
accept heaven, and Jesus Christ.
But you have to know, one day
they'll bulldoze the house away,
that it was unusual for you to tell the paramedics,
"Get me out of here."
So, I'm sorry, I was shaking.
We are all waiting for the day
when we see what's left of life
taken away.

Hide and Seek

Lemon cookies in the staff kitchen that were stolen by us. My guilt, sin, and I told you in the last days of college that we played hide-and-seek. I spread out my arms, stretching beyond earth. Guess what, I won. You will never guess my hiding spot, in the elevator, where no one uses this machine to get from one floor of the building to the next. Let me show you how it works: you step in, push a button, and the door will slide shut. The faces on the other side are never to be seen again. And maybe it is quicker to take the stairs sometimes, to avoid the thrilling ride of rising up and up. The same feeling you gave me, the way your tongue flicked the word "stole," like a light switch. When I saw you again, as if you were still in the bright light of the open kitchen, with a marble table top and a roaring stove. I again played hide-and-seek. Behind the sinks, the dishwasher, the pots and pans. I think you spotted me across the room. Something you would not admit. I won.

When We Leave

bottle of wine for sorrow,
pink liquid in tea cups,
scented bath bubbles,
closed shower curtains.

call on the fields,
lambs, and lost sheep,
gold coins,
a promise, a prodigal.

Fireworks Over the World

argue in dreams
secret of past sins
sick with a cough
stain red
somehow still had
sliced open wounds
sliding into oceans
of misbelief
the fireworks like little
schoolboys and girls
in patterned shirts
still scrawny

scanned the shimmer of skies
of serpents stealing
some part of beauty
scrambled
towards the exit sign
while hearing
Gods whisper
Him cooking

in kitchens with stones
shoes at the door
still just a child
sulked
broken from the world
watching the smoke
from pans
the

explosion of good

Prayer

Don't worry about anything; instead, pray about everything.

Philippians 4:6

One of Many Names

Lifter of waves, paving paths under the water,
salt drops, sand crest in my fist,
the beat, the breath
allowed my heart to break
when I watched the sun
go down
as if it were crashing into the ocean.
You are good in everything,
songs of folklore, fire, smoke
on the sands in the night, veiled in moonlight.
You are creator.
Power, pulling at my chest,
the 8.5 earthquake in Southern California,
You built those mountains with the bat of an eye,
break them down with your laughter.

The Way She Worshiped

Her knees
press against pine floor,
hands risen
as a flock of pigeons,
a white wedding
miracle to witness
the tears.
Notes of prayers
placed in a basket
passed an offering, a plea
to God.
those eyes close, tears a rhythmic
stream of memories
of mountains, forest, white swan
meddling her way through life.
All beauty discerns the pebbles, fallen trees,
summers to autumns, stone houses,
black beaks inside the berry bushes.
It is the silence when the wicker is passed,
hands pull out the paper.
A guitar strummed, heart thumped.
The simple act of praying,
saying it's okay to be small.
Insignificant to the scene behind
curtains,
the poison hidden in our hearts,
drumming, pattern of His
listening.

Fold Your Hands

Always in the night,
strumming of hearts heard through pillows.
Pounds, weights of what feels like days
that are kept secret.
This cry after shadows, after the long beating sleep,
till sun is almost awake.
This turmoil from self
is almost over.
I have a secret as well, it's been hidden under the mattress,
between overdue books and old shoeboxes.
That this life is already almost over,
you will be remembered for rings on your keys, your expression
when you bite your tongue.
But only a few until you are not–
a syllable, a wrinkle, remembered for your
sideways glance, heavy feet on the stairwell.
I cannot tell you the faces I have forgotten;
they are stick figures in my mind,
and I'm sorry for that.
It's only in the quiet when the world feels like there is no one,
when you look at the silver lake, moon, and fog.
The creature that is lurking, but it's too dark to see,
yet you feel, hear the crunch of leaves.
That's when you worry, it's all so obsolete.
So, endure, conjure ice in the winter,
poppies, daddy longlegs,
black bear sleeping away its life,
remember to fold your hands under the clear sky,
motion of a flock of geese.
Do not be afraid to cry in the night,
even alone.
Especially alone,
because what if, with great imagination,
your puffy eyes are stopped,
given away to depths of sorrow,
replaced to only gather the given love,
a gift, given like a saint in the night.
To be forgotten.
To be forgiven.

In a Whisper

Creature shifted its weight,
shoulder blades, back and forth
pull of muscle--the aggravation,
leather skin, tough and ready
to be patted with soil. Soul,
sinking inside, to which the eyes
blink, stare. He captures sugar cane,
bananas in wide woven baskets.
This living wonder, marvel
with thick, saggy, gray kneecaps,
snatching a snack with its nose
out of a tourist's hand.
And the ears, the blissful umbrella ears,
a fan, fashion accessory, to hear even
the small whispers.

Praise the Lord!
Praise the Lord from
the heavens! Praise
him from the skies!
Psalms 148:1

Dear Lord,

And let me say thank you,
enough as a feather,
a bundle of pencil shavings.
Collection of rocks, acorns,
lint in my pocket,
and still you are pleased.

Traffic

The horns honk, brakes, candy cane lights on the freeway. The fit of rage as if I were a toddler. But God, I have not gotten my way. I broke my back to see you in the back seat. There is a fire on the side of the motorway. Smoke and flame, a rubber neck, look, it's on the right. The world might be burning. There might be a crash, a spinning wheel, a tornado of dust coming from my mouth. All these things, God. Do you not see the damage done? Do you not hear the whispers on the radio, the voices from the world singing to you, to themselves, to their gods? And look, I'm running the red light. I'm slamming on the brakes. I'm taking my foot off the pedal.

And look, God. All the while, there in the parking lot, a father runs with his daughter in a shopping cart, all the world may be apart. But there are the mountains for their background, the sky, the sharp beak of the robin soaring past the exit sign.

And I have found a destination.

Peace in the Flame

My back to the heater, the wind knocking at my window
and the fires in LA burn bundles of memories made
from houses now crisp-broken open wounds.
I pray, in a world so defeated that those Palm trees
like necks on fire, cape of flames, does not discourage humanity
from hope. That the heat, this comfort
on my shoulders, will remind me that this place
is not safe. But in some way, somehow, light will erupt.

God Please: Moment of Memories

Don't let that ever-encompassing fear return.
You have climbed mountains, rushed past erupting
volcanoes, found and lost love. You have written things
from the heart and at the same time broken your own.
Please, let me beg, do not be disgusted with me,
I am only doing what I can. And I remember
that moment when the deer was ten feet away from me,
the nights I didn't sleep but was grateful to see the sunrise.
When my friends and I stayed outside the cafeteria at night.
God, don't let me pivot into that dark hole that I find so
comforting. Or lie on the wet grass alone, driving too close
to the edge of the highway. Lord, clean me. Cover the mud
on my eyes to clear my vision. Let me fly like the eagle I wrote
about in late December. Cover me when I do not want to
wake. Undo the moment when I spoke hideous words.
Keep me when all feels lost. Love me when I don't deserve it.

But God is so
rich in mercy,
and he loved us
so much.
Ephesians 2:4

Hear Me Pray

This is my quiet song
to God, to myself, to the beauty
of earth.

I am letting go, the seeds in the Magpie's
mouth, trees casting shadows
that birth

imaginary arms reaching out. I have waited
indoors for too long. But now I see the mystery,
the mirth

in the red sun of an eye, a white beak that speaks
the truth in rhythm. We are not alone, we hold all
this worth of a God-given earth.

My Prayer Includes You

I pray one day you'll hold me in the night,
that when I watched you watch TV,
engulfed in the blue chair, blue sweater--
my mind so captivated, turned to images
of the ocean, late afternoon parking lots,
shifting of shoulders.
Cold wonders in winter, plastic benches,
the pavement was broken, but we stepped over it.
sat in the little room with stained-glass windows,
rays of a spotlight on my face.
And I must tell you, the otters hold hands while sleeping,
bathed in radiant liquid--born to care for one another.
So I plead, remember me daily, whether it be the turquoise
bracelet I bound on your wrist under clear skies. Ripped jeans
or lingering words of my poetry held on paper left in your car.
Because the moon, the air, the winter where I fell in love are all
fountains falling in your direction.

When We Breathe with God

God, breathe for me
be the lullaby sung,
whisper of a bride
in the morning sun.
The candle lit for
the funeral, roses
budding before loves
last blink. The hum
from the TV static
as the old rest in peace,
staircase carrying
this young girl's feet.

Let me hear you
through the call
of the wolf
after its loss,
let me see you in
the butterfly on my shoe
in the garden room.
Wings fragile
as my prayer to you.
Let me be courageous
as I walk up this hill,
ice and rock, let me not
be alone.

Why

The question is not how we pray but why.
How often do we seek a maker?

Because often our perspective is wrong, we think the sharks are killing us,
but it's the mosquitoes, the malaria, the yellow fever
knocking humans off the planet like a quiet killer
ready to suck the blood, transfer a disease, and leave you to your demise.

These monsters populate the earth. They hunt just as much as the lion, the wolf.
The Inland Taipan, which can kill one hundred men with its venom.

I imagine the insect's tactic is to get us to believe that it's not so scary, only an irritation.
In the same way, busy days leave us too tired to search for more,
to not smile at the clerk in the grocery store,
hold a door open for some stranger,
to call that one loved one,
to pray for someone.

It is our view that causes us to forget
that we are the second most dangerous animals on the planet.

Buried inside are so many monsters, ready to hunt even more than the dogs with rabies,
the tapeworm, the jaw of the hippo, the feet of the elephant, the bite of the tiger.
And even they recognize the power they have.

You can pray for anything, and if you have faith, you will receive it.

Matthew 21:22

Soft prayer, answers as rain falls on the rooftop.
The bicycles left out again, and the water down the drainpipe.
Cups of coffee on the counter, wood stacked nearby. Smoke up the chimney.
Peace even in memory. Prayer handwritten and delivered.

Wind Chimes

Listen, I can hear
the wind chimes

same as the ones my sister
hung in our old room.

A bird and beating of a branch,
the trees speak

through the interpreter
of the wind.

These moments
I want to hear God.

Wonder what it feels like,
smells like chestnut,

smoke from the chimney
bringing up memories

by the light of the fire,
the Spirit in the swirl,

crackle of the ember
at my feet.

He's so sweet
a caramel popcorn,

salt, honey, and tea.
Yet, I know that voice

would not be as sweet-sounding
as my sister's chimes,

only an ultrasonic wave
some so willing to hear.

Ways God Speaks

God speaks through open doors, and passing thoughts,
in the way this song is whispering to me while I wait
in the entryway, gold embers and chestnut trunks
that still hold the photos of my mother's wedding, cut to
the cake, the puffy sleeves, and father's square glasses.
Miracles happen when she folds the white towels,
the blue bucket that I would hide under, illuminated
like I was again in the womb.
God spoke to me when I watched my mother sing
the sad Christmas song. That He was coming back
All along. That I was born out of sin, but it was still a miracle.

A Prayer at All Times

Linger here,
above the cherry blossoms
and your sweet soul, Lord
forever, is brighter than rays
that stains my face.

Capture me,
the weight of me sent to the clouds
is heavy in your arms,
to your voice,
softer than warm smiles.

Protect always,
as the seeds through rain, sun,
and isolation. Father, who sees
my arms reaching
do not loosen your embrace.

I also pray that
you will
understand the
incredible
greatness of God's
power for us who
believe him. This
is the same
mighty power
that raised Christ
from the dead.
Ephesians 1:19

The Roots

It starts at the roots, pushing into soil. Pulled to the sun.
God, I fear the wayward wind knocking on my door, the lack of
flowing fruit,
seeds dispersing.
I have become an enigma of prayer, mumble of words I need you to hear.
The glass scattered, the liquid infusing into wood, the world looking
into my eyes.
I dive into the droplets
the flower in the woman's hair,
my nature and yours.
The phone booth, the silence on the other end, the glass in my hand, my heart
quickening, you are not answering.
Yet always listening.

Kitchen and Garden Prayers

Putting away the dishes,
    everything in its place.

This glass plate here in the cupboard and the
    spoons in the drawer.

My folded hands, mumbles of the same words,
    "Will you please?"

Wash me completely, rinse, and
    Oh, why have things become?

When prayer can be like gardening,
    new greens sprouting.

My hands in the dirt of things, messy,
    but with every weed

Pulled. There is room for growth, for flowers,
    daisies, blooming like

words not having to be honey, but they
    ease their way from lips,

the eagerness to beg, knees deep in the soil
    of my child-like cries.

Polaroid on Valentine's Day

You think we won't find a better picture than the Polaroid
taken on Valentine's Day.
It's as if you prayed for sunset, periwinkle cirrus clouds,
the ground squirrels, rabbits,
as if there are fields of saffron, silk memories of
my prayers that you would lean into me.

Bonsai Cascade

dying leaves of a bonsai cascade
left in overgrowth.
Behind the yellow fence
where dogs will chew its branches,
question the significance underlying
lives hidden in forest, years of broken
backs   bones in the eyes of woman.

The rugged terrain turned on its side,
fatten to the outermost worlds,
summits to the wicker   wood
that builds the houses, those men   women
clamor in   question God's motives.

Moves through the path   roads   truckloads
of summer, spring, and mountain plants
to place in the back of your home.
And when it does not grow,
let your resilient body   mind remember
God's prayer to you.

The work   strength in every limb.
Beauty   bliss assurance that the wobbly
walk of your infant feet will be brought up
under the weight   tug of Christ.
The bonsai cascade, a fountain.

Your eyes will
see the king in
all his splendor,
and you will see
a land that
stretches into the
distance.
Isaiah 33:17

Questions to Myself

Jot and tittle.
Grand canyon of you,

in begrimed rain.
mouthful.

What does your pen write?

It says, "God be near to me."
In mud mouths, washed
in summer's love.

Prayed for My Arrival

All pink ribbon,
pastel bows,
patterned crystals,
purple cribs,
pacifiers, roses.
She folds into
chariot, her bed,
flushed strawberry nose.
Whispers as the bat of an eye,
bold convictions and demands,
so God, so willing.
Flesh like seeds
swells in mother's belly,
bobs,
bounces,
an apple of joy.
And with curiosity,
she prayed for me daily,
naked knees,
porcelain ruby flooring.
Jolts of confetti
in the sore of her stomach
when she discovered I was a girl.
Wooden spoon,
yellow milk,
broken yoke of now daily
courage carved in the arms,
where head resides,
pile of laundry,
private blemish,
of a tomato-faced baby
built to beg, cry,
pound her fist
until her convictions and bold demands,
so God, so willing.

How He's Waiting

we pray
because we don't know what else to call.
Last summer, rough, raw, roaring   beat

                                                    of my heart.

knows that there is no one else who truly listens
 to me.

God,
forgive me, you let the ringlets of my sin run down,
carry like the time I sat watching the pigeons eat bread
on the cement. Until all was gone.

Until dead roses raise their heads, your body
beaten, a rodent on the side of the road.
Yet, you find your way into my thoughts,

drops of mercy, nearly making their way up to my mouth
to pour out praise. The rose, she with no water, no root, nothing
but her name, breaths.

Praise the Lord; praise God our savior! For each day he carries us in his arms. Psalms 68:19

www.ingramcontent.com/pod-product-compliance
Lightning Source LLC
LaVergne TN
LVHW020650100826
845148LV00012B/2410

* 9 7 9 8 3 8 5 2 7 3 6 9 0 *